DO DAD

For the dads with the kids that won't close their eyes or pillow their heads, who lay there awake with thoughts in their beds.

PROVERBS 22:6, PSALM 19:14

Remember THE doer that did do what he'd said, and said what he'd do, if it were his choice instead?

Psalm 34:18

He'd seen so many Sad, Indifferent, Depressed, with a frown looking down, never looking up instead.

Psalm 14:1

Over time, over questions of doing, before going to bed.

Ephesians 6:12

He Proped up His Head " Just wait one moment keep that light on!" he said.

1 JOHN 1-10, Psalm 8:3

A doer does things, which nobody
does or did before.

LUKE 1:37

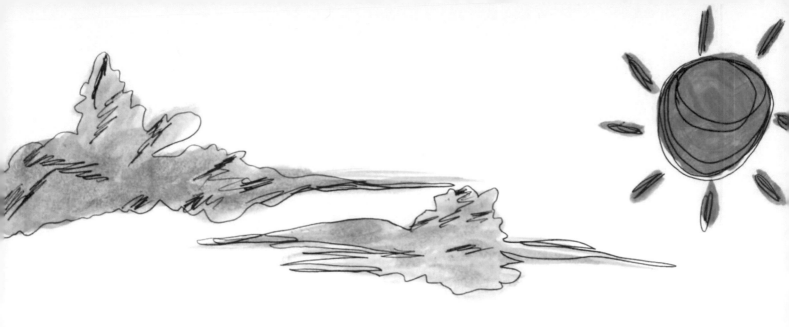

Before they got up or wipe their eyes of the mud, no matter the cost the sweat or the blood.

John 16:33   Psalm 37:20-24

A doer does right over the wrong, even
if painful to sing, he'll sing along.

REVELATION 19:6

Nothing a stitch or a patch cannot fix. A doer corrects the errors of his wavs!

LUKE 9:1-27

And spends quality time looking at
the now and the how, of a day.

Psalm 1:2, Joshua 1:18 KJV, Psalm 119:11

A doer forges forward, and bares all things in LOVE, even the crummy, most awful, unthinkable blot of sud.

Romans 3:1-23

Mark 10:1-9, 1Corinthians 16:13, Romans 5:2
Mathew 10:19

So seeing the doer had done what he'd done. I did what I did, and I went where he'd gone, and begun.

Romans 10:1-13

"So now what is there to do,
now that I'm spent?"

QUESTIONS...

He started to lose count of the Questions
that popped up in his head,

Matthew 6:20-34

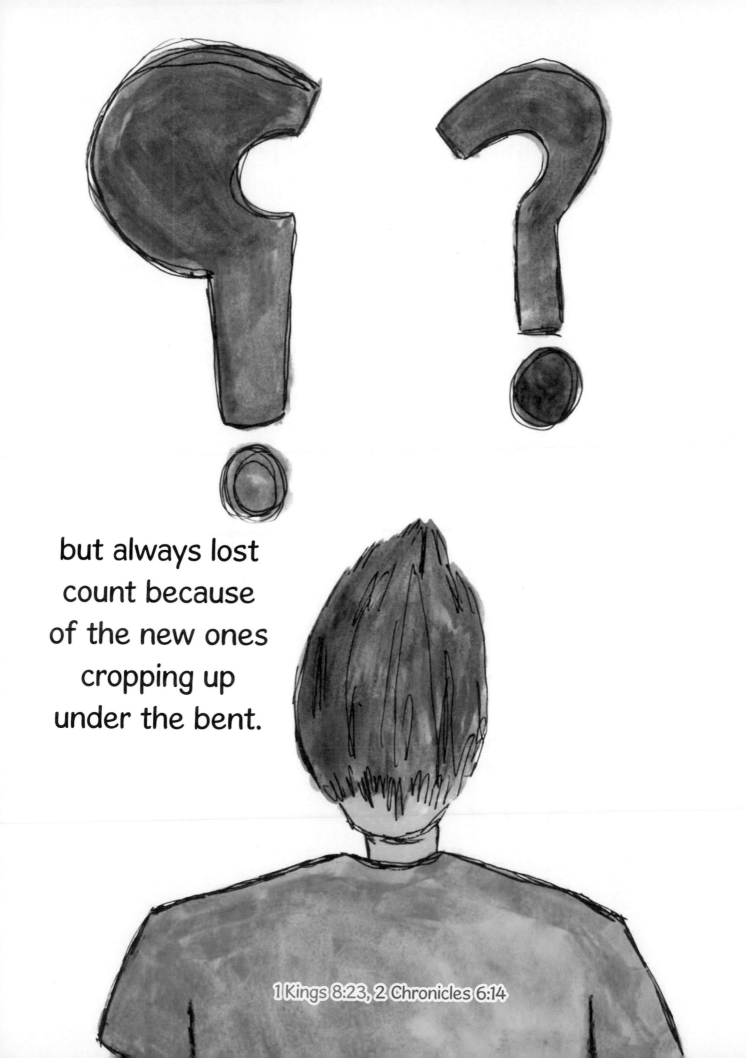

but always lost count because of the new ones cropping up under the bent.

1 Kings 8:23, 2 Chronicles 6:14

Some looked like others and other looked like the same one. Questions of all kinds, some big and some small, some short and some tall.

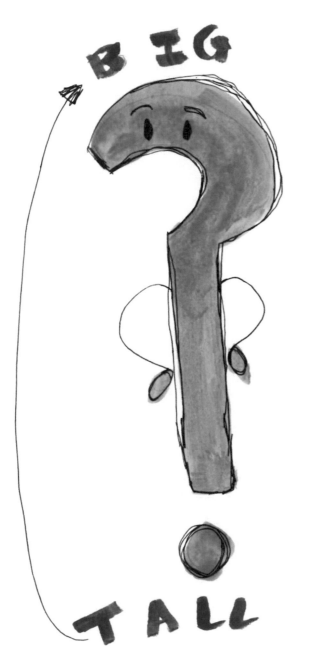

1 Corinthians 4:1-2, 1Peter 4:1-11

https:// wwww.focusonthefamily.com/faith/the-truth-project/

John 14:1-6

Others ran away down the hall.

LUKE 8:1-18, MATTHEW 7:24-27, Hebrews 11:6

Yes, fun can get messy!

But, CLEAN IT UP, we can.

Philippians 4:13

That's what he's good at, the doer.

Luke 10:37, Mattew 28:16-20, Acts 2:42, Romans 16:17, Johb 1:10

Yes, you've seen them
in action before.

2 chronicles 7:14

There is no fun in a mess if
the learning's a chore.

JAMES 1:12,

Don't fire the help or call in for
more, make cleaning FUN!

That's what it's for, 'Fun!' that is.

1 Peter 3:15

Doers do right and do write all the more. Call in to action all those good doers once more, Vote on the actions that help clean up the floor.

Instead of those old spend'lers that spend,

PSALM 91:2

till they come back asking for more.

Then the doer remembered what a good doer once did.

ISAIAH 35:6, PROVERBS 12:28 PROVERBS 18:21, Ephesians 2:8

That doer was Dad
and cleaned up,
is what he did!

Romans 1:17, Galatians 3:11

Cleaned up, is what to do, as a good doer once did. "There's a moment a miss amongst all that I'd read, while doing what a doer once did."

Hebrews 13:9, Jeremiah 17:9

A miss match. A miss hap, perhaps.

2 Timothy 1:7

ERROR
SYSTEM STUCK

A cog in the wheel?
Something has bent
all the props and
melted the seal.

The heat
tempered up
throughout the
whole deal.

Romans 8:28

PONDER

DOER

The time came to
carefully consider,
ponder, then review!

CONCIDER

What would a doer do?

http://www.kendrickbrotherscatalogue.com/courageous/

Not just lumped up
over upon dread or
stumbled upon over
his or her head,

But Doing it over and over, the right way on purpose instead.

That a boy!
That a girl!

Psalm 4:8, Proverbs 3:24, Proverbs 10:5, Ecclesiastes 5:12, Daniel 12:2, John 11:11, 1 Corinthians 11:30

Now let's get you to your bed. With your eyes all closed up and you curled up tight and warm, with sweet dreams of the doing you'll do, when the

doers are done and YOU!,
take off to do what they
haven't yet done and more.

James 1:23–25, 1 Corinthians 13:12, Revelation 2:5, 1 Corinthians 3:18, Proverbs 27.

The Doer their DAD.

Psalm 119:105

Printed in the United States
by Baker & Taylor Publisher Services